Published in 2023
First published in the UK by THP Kidz Zone
An imprint of Tamarind Hill Press Limited
Newton Aycliffe, County Durham, DL5 6XP
Copyrights © THP Kidz Zone
All rights reserved

Written by Petrina Frost

ISBN Paperback: 978-1-915161-50-5

Printed and manufactured by Lightning Source LLC

LEBO LOVES YOGA

By Petrina Frost

This book belongs to:

_____

_____

Hi, my name is Lebo and I love practising yoga.

I learned how to be mindful and calm by practising yoga with my grandmother, and I want to share this knowledge with you.

First, let's try the prayer pose.

Place your hands together at your heart and take a deep breath.

You will feel a sense of peace and calm wash over you.

Now, let's try the second pose. It's not so hard. It's like crawling around when you play.

Try the cow pose.
Get down on all fours and stretch your back.

You will feel a sense of relief and openness.

Let's stretch our bodies a little more.

Give the downward facing dog pose a go. Lift your hips up towards the sky and stretch your arms and legs.

You'll feel strong and grounded, like a tree planted deep into the earth.

As we continue to practice, let me show you new poses...

Like the extended triangle and standing bow.

Each pose challenges our bodies and helps us focus our minds on the present moment.

We can also try poses like the standing hand to toe pose and triangle pose.

They both require balance and concentration.

We might wobble at first, but with practise, we can become steadier and more confident.

With each pose, you and I will feel more peaceful and centred.

We'll start to feel like superheroes.

Now, let's learn the warrior pose, which helps us feel strong and brave.

Practising yoga and mindfulness can help us stay calm and focused, even when we face new challenges or fears.

You might feel some aches and pains on your first day, but keep on going, in time you will feel okay.

I have benefited from practising yoga, and so can you.

Let's try the chair pose, feeling our legs and arms stretch as we bend our knees and raise our hands towards the sky.

We'll feel light and free, ready to take on any challenge that comes our way.

And now that we are feeling big and strong, let's try the tree pose.

Stand on one foot and feel the breeze brush against your face.

You will feel grounded and stable, like the roots of a tree spreading deep into the ground.

Let's spend a couple of minutes enjoying some peace and quiet in your mind. Get into lotus position, the final pose.

Sit cross legged with your hands resting on your knees like me.

You'll feel a deep sense of peace and contentment.

By practising yoga and mindfulness, you and I can learn to be more mindful, calm, and happy.

Practise with me every day, and we'll feel like we can face any challenge that comes our way with a calm and centred mind.

Namaste.

www.ingramcontent.com/pod-product-compliance
Lightning Source LLC
Chambersburg PA
CBHW051322110526
44590CB00031B/4439